AGONY

S ADARSH

Copyright © S Adarsh
All Rights Reserved.

to the world...

Contents

Preface

Everything that happens for a reason maybe true but the reason cannot be everything that happens,

Some people may call it as coincidence or destiny,

but the reality is life is running in live.

This is the world of poems and quotes which you can relate with your life.

SHE

I am in a prison of pain,
Where all my feelings are arrested.
The dreams experience her,
But reality never tried it.
She's like a star in the sky,
But never realises when she's gonna stay and when she
will fall.

FEAR

I never thought the affection, which I have on her
Will leave me in rejection.
Maybe the attention was low,
So the intention became high.
Then her eyes showed the lies,
And my fears became the tears.

STAND BY

I drenched in rain,
with full of pain.
Where I blindly believed one,
And gently left me alone.
Anyway flashback was on my eyes,
Maybe her comeback is just a lies.

OUTCAST

I was lonely in the lovely world.
Where I got Friendship gain,
Which left me in Hardship pain.
Maybe i was blind,
So they left me in behind.
I made them mingle,
But they left me in single.

DELETERIOUS

smoking a cigarette daily and Loving a girl truly
Are actually same.
The only difference is
Smoking is injurious to lungs,
Love is injurious to heart.

SWEEP

"Love is like a virus"
The only difference is
Virus spreads through air
And
Love spreads through hearts.

RETRACT

I have seen her,
Instead I should have seen somewhere else .
I shouldn't have met her,
Instead I should have not met any other.
I shouldn't have talk to her,
Instead I should have talk to someother .
I should haven't think about her,
Instead I should completely forget her.

UNFOLDING

"Every heart has a pain"
"Every pain has a feeling"
"Every feeling has a suffering"

THROW BACK

"The reality of my love is
Highlight of your character"

OBLITERATE

"The words came from you was forgiven"
But not
"Forgotten"

DISCERN

"*We never realize the love of our dear ones when they are with us*"
"*When they are far,*
We yearn their love".

CADENCE

"Time is like a girl"
It doesn't wait for us,
But
We wait for it.

APPRISE

"Soul tells us past
Heart tells us present
Mind tells us future"

DEMENTED

Whenever I come too closer to her,she goes far from me,
Whenever I go far from her,she comes too closer to me.

SCARCELY

"Crying is only way",

when your eye speaks when your heart is hurted.

GOSPEL

*"Hurt them with your truths,
Not with lies.*

WITHDRAW

"Never ever care someone for more"
Because
One day they will leave you for sure.

BIAS

When reality of love gets stronger,
The partiality of friendship becomes weaker.

TORMENT

"Pain of love kills" ,
But
"Gain of friends lives.

THE END

"Life without a women "
Is
"Darkness without the lights"

live is like a swing

never tell someone to push

push yourself.